A BUNCH
OF
STICKS

A COLLECTION OF POEMS AND RECOLLECTIONS

By David R Hamber

© Copyright 2006 David Hamber.
All rights reserved. No part of this publication may be reproduced, stored in a retrieval system, or transmitted, in any form or by any means, electronic, mechanical, photocopying, recording, or otherwise, without the written prior permission of the author.

Note for Librarians: A cataloguing record for this book is available from Library and Archives Canada at www.collectionscanada.ca/amicus/index-e.html
ISBN 1-4120-7928-4

Printed on paper with minimum 30% recycled fibre. Trafford's print shop runs on "green energy" from solar, wind and other environmentally-friendly power sources.

Offices in Canada, USA, Ireland and UK

This book was published *on-demand* in cooperation with Trafford Publishing. On-demand publishing is a unique process and service of making a book available for retail sale to the public taking advantage of on-demand manufacturing and Internet marketing. On-demand publishing includes promotions, retail sales, manufacturing, order fulfilment, accounting and collecting royalties on behalf of the author.

Book sales for North America and international:
Trafford Publishing, 6E–2333 Government St.,
Victoria, BC v8t 4p4 CANADA
phone 250 383 6864 (toll-free 1 888 232 4444)
fax 250 383 6804; email to orders@trafford.com

Book sales in Europe:
Trafford Publishing (UK) Limited, 9 Park End Street, 2nd Floor
Oxford, UK ox1 1HH UNITED KINGDOM
phone 44 (0)1865 722 113 (local rate 0845 230 9601)
facsimile 44 (0)1865 722 868; info.uk@trafford.com

Order online at:
trafford.com/05-2826

10 9 8 7 6 5 4 3 2

Part of the Hamber family in Cranes Farm Road Nevendon Essex in the summer of 1948

Kenny Reid Cousin Chris Howard Dennis Dorothy
Mary   David   William

The author and his sister Mary at the same spot 57 years later.

Acknowledgements

First to my mother Jesse May Bentley and father Reginald Hugh Hamber for without them I would not have been. Also my dear brothers, sisters, wives and children. And of course my friends who all made life so very interesting.

David R Hamber Ohio USA 2005.

Contents

Page	
6	Introduction
7	A Bunch of Sticks
9	The Motor Car
10	God Save The King
12	Billericay
15	A Change of Clothes
16	A Sailor's Life
18	Solvig
20	Gem
21	Conscience
23	Earning or Learning
25	Kent
26	The Family Photo
27	Ye-Old Kitchen
28	The Modern Kitchen
29	My Wife
31	Olympics 2000
32	The Plough 1950's
34	The Plough 1960's
36	Time Gentlemen Please
38	The Shed
41	When I Was Bad
42	Lynher
44	The Bench
45	The Sniper
46	Positively Negative
47	The Last Hare
49	The Village
50	The English

Introduction.

In the days before television it was either the radio or reading that kept you occupied on a wet and windy day, that, or the sound of an elder brother or sister reciting a piece of poetry. It was thought important to learn at least one all the way through and praise was heaped on he or she for remembering the lines. Haunted still today by that memory, I guess my love of poetry comes just as a piece of music reminds me of my happy childhood.

English was the master and London the classroom where poets met and were applauded by others for a line or a verse. Many tried hard to find the words to express their feelings and some would be never forgotten, etched on minds forever in future years by teachers who would try hard to get you to orate them. Some wrote just one, and tried even harder to better it, yet there were those like Rudyard Kipling whose hand produced so many it is difficult to have a favourite.

While Europe produced the music of the ages, England, a more vocal society, was freer to speak out loud. William Wordsworth (a bit of a revolutionary in his younger days) believed France was the place to be, he was lucky to flee home and write 'Daffodils' from the safety of the Lake District. It is the one poem more than all others for which he is remembered. Such it was with so many, Walter de la Mare's 'The Listeners', Thomas Hood's 'I remember, I remember', Alfred Noyes 'The Highwayman'. Frost, Tennyson, Masefield, Brooke, Betjeman and so many more plied their art and hand at writing verse.

Who could better them? None could and in my opinion none ever will. They left us with a longing to leave something behind that will be judged in future years and by future generations. I had a ten-year burst at writing, wishing to leave something of me behind other than a few photographs that say very little. In this small book I have put together some I think might be acceptable.

David Robert Hamber Oct 2005 Ohio U.S.A.

Sticks

Counting my mother and father, cousins, uncle and aunt, 20 of us lived down Cranes Farm Road, Nevendon, in a lane that held no more than 30 at the most. We played together, laughed together and watched out for each.

While Adolf Hitler sat in his bunker wondering what the hell went wrong, England was producing another load of 'Tommies' for the trenches, till. The message came from higher up saying 'Reg - stop - We have won - stop - Don't need any more - stop - So stop it - stop!' - Love George -stop!

The chance to make the old Aesop fable come true can so easily be missed. In a family containing seven boys, seven sticks can be a right little bundle to break. The trouble was some never listened to our mother when she told them of the old Greeks fable, yet in times of trouble, I have experienced its worth.

Aesop lived 2,500 years ago and I just wonder how many families had the chance to listen to the wise words of advice and acted on them! Wise words from a wise mother or father can fall on deaf ears I'm afraid.

A Bunch of Sticks

Oh what beauty, did they once behold,
Who did not listen, to wise words told,
About the fable, about the sticks,
About the road, the individual picks.

Comes the sadness, from such joy!
Comes the man, once the boy,
Came the chance, to make your mark,
Once the fire, now but a spark!

So much struggle, so much sacrifice,
So much for love, so much for advice,
There lies the rub, there lies the rue,
There lies the story, that never came true!

Oh behold my beautiful boys, what sacrifices were made,
Your picture stands there to remind me, of the terrible price that we paid.
Will you be like chafe to the winnower, I fear like me you may drift,
When your hearts and minds are confused, to others your love could shift.
The struggle, the pain to deliver you, a bundle of such little joys,
But what will you grow in to as men, will you forget who you were as boys.

Never forget where you came from, you that I loved so dear,
It is too late I know now to listen, for when did children ever hear?
Remember the last shall come first, hear what youngest did say,
For foolish words first spoken, may come to assist one day.
They will never forgive or forget you; it's harder for them to climb,
The respect you first gave them, will long be remembered in time!

Oh behold my beautiful children, one glimpse at life and it's gone,
Never let another come between you, together you'll always be strong,
Or will the tears that so hurt my eyes, fester like that very thorn,
Like the boy who remembers that day, from the socket his eye was torn.
And shall I remember for a moment, this picture and just the scene,
Of what you were as children, and as men, what you might have been.

DRH March 2002.

The Motor Car

Before the love affair seduced, when roads were then a track,
Before the people were reduced, to a life where you can't look back.
The pace was set by a man or a horse, along Tow-path Canal,
It was the way of life of course, by the scene so banal.
Through Country side at a steady pace, observed by the artists eye,
Hauling barges with a certain grace, for a nation to supply.
It was Commerce, it was trade, until a bloody train got made!

Came the Navvies in a scurry, with their shovels and their picks,
Like swarms of ants in a hurry English, Taffys and Micks.
From cuttings to hide from his lordship eye, the monster spitting fire and steam,
They built embankments that a train could fly, over gorges where wound the stream.
It was nothing but muscle and brawn, from the Navvies that laid the track,
While Canals their days would mourn, the day England could never go back!
It was commerce; it was trade, until the bloody car got made!

In traffic jams ten miles long, sit the people with their engines on,
Next to the truck with his load now late, nothing he can do but sit and wait.
Slowly as both come to the boil, laughing at us are those in oil,
So our love affair with the motor car, is a stop and go affair thus far,
Next to the truck with its heavy load, fighting for space on crowded road,
No place to turn you're in a Cul-de Sac and England now can never go back!
It was commerce, it was trade, the day some one saw money made!

DRH July 2002

The King

The British Empire, like that of the Mongols, was never defeated but was dissolved into nations, who now control their own destiny. When history writes of its achievements (and it will take some time to admit it) they will write of law and order first, how under the protection of its flag the 90 counties sat safe, like that of the great Kahns. All subjects revered our Kings and our Queens. Sadly, the chipping away at our Royalty is slowly eroding its importance and the media is trying its best to undermine its need. A very fine hair holds the sword that hangs over the head and those that would love it to fall believe a President better than a King.

God Save The King

A good man with all he could ask for, that could never have it taken away,
A man with a conscience and the ability, to hear what his subjects do say.
That when he heard their grievance, be as fair and as honest as he can,
Why such a man will be followed by all, even the guilty man!

Such a man is needed more than ever, today where despots are bred.
Those with neither rhyme nor reason, but to cause trouble with that tongue in their head.
And those Parliamentary thick-heads, who put all but themselves firmly down,
They are looking for a way to join Europe, but must first do away with the crown.

There's a war going on in our country, to take from our monarch his might.
By the dogs that just won't come to 'heel', whose bark is worse than his bite.
They know our liege lord is vulnerable, they know the best place to strike,
They are taking away his defences, the Lords and the Ladies and the like.

They wish to change our England, which has survived for a thousand years,
And not so much as a sword was raised, by one of his most loyal peers.
Men in suits not of armour, walked amongst them and said to them "Yield!"
Then marched away the Kings own men, stripped of ermine, honour, and shield.

Gone went the crowns of Europe, gone because they could not hear,
The cries out for help from their subjects, who never had a word in his ear.
He was locked up tight in his castle, by advisors who said all was well!
And were the first to leave by the back door, just before the castle it fell!

These are the people without faces, that made their escape in the dark,
They are now the Kings of their country, with a bite much worse than their bark.
They don't like to see our England, with its Earls, its Lordships and Knights,
And worst is the thought that our armies, swear to stand by their King when he fights.

Every nation must have a leader, and a leader with his nation in his heart,
But how can a leader lead a nation, when that idea is to tear it apart?
Is what's on their mind any better, will we love our neighbours now for sure?
By signing some documentation, will it mean there will never be war?

Will the Gaul, the Frank and the Hun, the Scythian and all Euro races,
Bury their tribal differences, with a handshake and a smile on their faces.
When rogues can't influence fools anymore, and inquisitions do really cease,
When the entire world respects the one God, maybe there will be peace.

If for ten thousand years two half brothers, Isaac and Ishmael's lot,
Have been fighting then and today, over who got his share of what.
Can you honestly ask us to believe, that the rest of the scattered tribes,
Will trust the hand of the blind again, and do as another fool abides.

Is England ready to swap, a sackful of Ferrets for a King?
Ready to cash in their inheritance, for a very uncertain thing?
We may not have our Empire, on which the sun never set,
Are we ready to exchange our King, when you can see what without one you get?

No! Before they strip our King of his power, to speak for us in high places,
To give away his influence, to fools with far lesser graces.
Let us remember what we're asked to forget, that as a nation we never did a thing,
And all that England ever achieved, was due totally to a rotten old King!

DRH December 1999

My home town

Billericay, my old home town. I was raised here from the early 50's, and at a time when plans were in the heads of those determined to destroy all that I once knew. Labour Government had demanded that certain areas be made available for the likes of us in need to be housed on 'Estates'. Ours was at South Green, but slowly and surely others came and Billericay heard the voices of those with their London accents replacing the Essex one with - "Know what I mean mate?" One would have to travel a long way now to hear that Essex sound - probably in time too!

The memories of my old town are still with me, like some lost love affair of sweet youth you hope not to meet in old age due to the broken image you wish to hold on to. It was once a market town whose high street hung on to fine old buildings, one of which my brothers and I pulled down and rebuilt to its original grandeur. 'Bleak House'. A great pity others had not the same sympathetic treatment.

Billericay

Give me a soft pillow, give me a warm snug bed,
Free me of all thoughts, that run through my head.
Let me quietly drift back, to my childhood teens,
Surrounded by a picture, of Billericay scenes.

I shall walk to Lake Meadows, from my home in South Green,
Where on every Sunday, family gatherings could be seen.
Scattered round its grassy banks, comes that summer sound,
Of those living far from the sea, yet water they have found.
Laughing, squealing children, some their eyes full of tears,
Romped in shallow paddling pools, moms and dads little dears.
There sleeps a man in his deckchair, the Sunday paper done,
It covers now his tiredness, his face from the heat of the sun!

Cheese and tomato sandwich, a flask of rather warm tea,
Strawberry jam on crusty bread, spread out under a shady tree.
A Cucumber from the garden, a small bottle of fizzy lemonade,
A shout coming from someone's mother, that lunch is being made!
And thankful children eating all, breathless from the game,
Knew there would be nothing more, till home and dinner came.
For Sunday then was a day of rest, and for everyone it meant,
That even if you had a penny, a penny could not be spent!

Young girls with the coming of age, eluding their moms and dads,
Came passing ever closer, a bunch of some likely lads!
If told to come and join 'em, they would giggle and turn away,
Watch them walk around the lake, slowing down to pass your way.
Here and there is a family group, on a rowboat, one you could hire,
A young Jack-Tar, flexing his muscles, in full view of his desire!
And upon a bank two lovers lay, stirred by the heat of the day,
Wishing for that moment when, the crowds would go away.
By late afternoon, and none too soon, for those with their sun-burnt faces,
It's time to pack your things, till another Sunday brings, people thankful for very small graces!

Let me now walk in to town, from 36 Hickstars Lane,
Up 'Bell Hill' at a good pace, past the old Mill again.
You might hear the bus a-coming, the dear old 251,
Out from Southend to London, on the Wood Green run.

I am off to meet my pals now, some of my old school friends,
It was years before the girls, and for some the friendship ends.
It is that time for the Carnival show, the towns yearly Fair,
With its smartly marching brass bands, with a strong military air!
There are stalls, there are floats, there are the Carnival Queens,
Her princesses waving gaily and too, the might just have beens!
And there goes Lt Ferris, with his Air Cadets,
Those left of the 'Few', in their blue Berets.
The Old Guard and the new, the Civil Defence,
Adding to the scene, still of some consequence.

Let me mingle with the crowd, the young and the old,
Faces that I knew so well, but their names never told.
It is Candyfloss, Punch and Judy tents,
Merry-go-rounds, and manly events.
A cork in a gun, boxes of sweets,
Weighed down with pennies, by the man that cheats!
Dodgem cars, where a change for a pound,
Got you a half-crown short, palmed off by a hound!
And to top all off, there was the Carnival dance,
In The Archer Hall, without a girl for a dance!

Quiet was the High Street, on a winter's night,
Not old enough to drink, or mad enough to fight.
Those shapes that you saw, just walking about,
You knew who they were, so gave 'em a shout!
It was either 'The Ritz', or the Snooker hall,
A very old film, or just acting the fool!
There was no Chinese food then, no Indian Vindaloo,
Just 'Goodspeeds' Fish & Chips, Nine pence for the two.
And when it got real late, you were bound to meet,
An 'Ox' of a man on patrol, out there on his beat!
Sergeant Bell you respected, not just for his size,
But by the arm on your shoulder, and the look in his eyes!
A gentle giant of a man he was, whose hobby was tame rabbits,
Or clipping the ear of the cheeky lad, or boys with bad habits.

A man who walks out more than one pair of shoes,
Sees life at the pace he wishes too choose.
He stops when he likes, to chat in a way,
What a man in a car, has no time to say!

It hurts when you return to the place where you grew,
Where not a face in the crowd is of one that you knew.
Fields too in which I ran now house the total stranger,
Not a soul said enough is enough nor visualized the danger.
From South Green to Queens Park from Burstead North to Stock,
Returning Billericians were in for quite a shock!
From The Crown to The Rising Sun this old market town,
Saw prices going up and only buildings coming down.
For the land of my youth where my memory still roams,
Is now but a pile of bricks in a Cul-de-sac of homes!

My old hometown and its market street,
Saw once the Roman march on his feet.
Saw the Angles the Saxons and the Jutes,
Carving out a place to put down some roots.
As a young boy it was plain I had seen,
The last of an England as it must have been.
Though invaders did come none were by far,
More destructive than the man and his motor car.

DRH June 2000

A Change of Clothes

Once new were the clothes now neatly pressed,
Ready for school then I was dressed.
Collars turned on a bleached white shirt,
Trousers scrubbed of farmyard dirt.
In Jacket and in Jumper too,
Where once inside my brothers grew.
Room for me to move and spread,
Worn all day, till time for bed!

So off I went down Cranes Farm lane,
With thoughts of never seeing home again.
Past the meadow where grazing herd,
Shared its patch with Rabbit and bird.
Thud! Thud! Thud! in timely beat,
In boots that saw my brothers feet.
So reluctantly I would be led,
To a place I learned to dread!

I saw no point to that red brick place,
That held no sympathetic face,
No kindly words, all strict demands,
Or threats to break you to commands.
Where what I wore, did not seem bad,
Till I saw what others had.
The beauty seen by such eyes,
Did stop the day they wished me wise.

Why did I have to go to school?
Why did they wish me not a fool?
Why did I have to learn to read?
At five, really was there a need?
I liked not teachers nor their trick,
Refused to learn arithmetic.
For I was young, and they did show,
What you become when you do grow!

DRH June 1994

So many memories

Having had some experience of sea life aboard a sailing boat, the thoughts that one has when you're not sure if you shall survive the storm and what made you wish for a time at sea. They do come to you and are very real. Then, a blue sea replaces the blackness of night, a nice breeze and a bone in her teeth and you know. The sea is a place to make you realize how insignificant you are, how terribly vulnerable and just how close death awaits the unwary. You form a mutual friendship with a kind of person that after some years can never be broken. Those living with their feet nailed to the land only experience life knowing tomorrow brings yet another day, boring as that may be, but for those out there sailing, or coming to anchor, they form a certain respect for each.

A Sailors Life

Wrapped up in his bunk at night, on a wind tossed stormy sea,
The sailor lays his weary head, just thoughts for company.
All's snug down, all is tight, there's no more they can do,
Bilges are pumped out and dry, and manned while the tempest blew.

He chose this life a sailor's life, adventures by the score,
When he saw ships leaving the port, for some far distant shore.
Where Palm trees grew and trade winds blew, and fortunes came from plunder,
But not tonight his thoughts are of home, when his ship she may go under.

Somewhere on that great dark Ocean, before the following wave,
His little ship a mere coffin now, being tossed on a watery grave.
He made himself a promise again, "No more at sea I'll vow!"
But if he'd kept his promises then, he'd not be where he is now.

He'd been at sea now many a year, without much of a care in sight,
But there was something in that hollow wind, that spoke to him tonight.
He lay there thinking of others, at home with all they desire,
A wife, a family, roof over their head, to tend not a ship but a fire.

What made him yearn for the sea, the salt that runs in his blood?
He thought how he'd watched 'em come and go, in and out on the flood.
Down by the old salty river, dreaming with his head in his hands,
Wondering what he was a-missing, that only he now understands.

He lay back and he remembered, how all of his wishes came true,
Yet now he wished to be home again, as above him the tempest blew.
But would he be happy with such a life, even though he may now agree,
Complaining about worldly possessions, then complaining they wont set him free?

A man and his troubles are parted, when tired heads and pillows meet,
But he awoke to the shout of "All hands on deck", and the sound of running feet!
There was no time to think or worry, as busy hands know what to do,
Each pin memorized, and what it supplied, aloft where the block it ran through!

"Make sail on her!" came down the orders, and orders is what sailors obey,
It could only be what he failed to see, a lee shore but who could say?
Above him the topsail exploded, as gaskets were loosed and let go,
What our skipper had in mind, the mate would soon let us know.

Two men at the helm were ordered, and orders to the mate were cast,
Sturdy hands too as the mighty strain, was carried from sail yard to mast.
To club-haul her round was the order, as the starboard tack she drew,
If she 'missed stays' we were finished, him, her, and the crew!

We passed a cable outside her, hauling it back to the head,
With the hope and scope to strike bottom, no time for swinging the lead.
With an anchor and axe at the ready, to part with it when given the shout,
To hold long enough without parting, in the hope to put her about.

Twas a rainy squall that made it plain to us all, that the wind had started to shift,
The Port-tack now was the problem, since the kedge had been cut adrift.
"Every man for himself!" said the skipper; "Each man for himself!" came the call,
"The Port-tack that once would have saved us, is now surely death to us all!"

Those hands that were rarely his own, did all that his masters did say,
Were paid off then, not needed again, so he put them together to pray!
"Forgive me oh Lord if I haven't, done all you desired of me,
Excuses for right when I know I did wrong, could be down to some bad company.
My hands that have shown some anger, yet believed they were always fair,
I put them together right now, to be led by my maker up there!"

Never a Saint nor a sinner, has retuned with what he can expect,
Your life is yours for the making, till it comes for the time to collect.
He looked at his mates all around him, and good mates they had been too,
Not one good swimmer among 'em, and that went for him he knew.

A man can say much of himself, with a pint of beer in his hand,
But the sea will soon show he is not, what he thinks he is on the land.
Men can spend their life not knowing, what life holds for them in store,
They think they have good mates too, yet know not what good mates are for.

None will forget that time in their lives, the only time they were ever free,
To sail with a good breeze behind 'em, in the best of the best company
They are what make life worth living, and grateful he'd been given that chance,
For where but at sea dies the sailor, and he gave them all a last glance.

DRH. August 1992

Such a trim little craft says I

The year was 1967/8 and from the bank overlooking the Blackwater at Heybridge Basin, my brother and I watched this pretty little Ketch make her way up the river. She eventually came alongside in the lock. It was love at first sight, I ached so much it hurt. Never was I so struck by so much longing as on that day and never would I imagine that in the near future could I ever be part of that world. I guess, that if you want something so much - anything is possible.

Solvig

The name on the stern said 'Solvig', I'd watched her making her way,
Coming up the river Blackwater, in the still of a cold winter's day.
Not breath of wind in the grey sky, riding high on the flooding tide,
The gates of the lock were open, hard a-starboard she came alongside.

Soon enough she was inside the Basin, in with the barges and craft,
All rattled down and canvas furled, with her wheel and dodger back aft.
She was a pretty little Baltic Trader, built for the open sea,
Built for those with a longing, built for the likes of me!

The skipper was ashore in a moment, a small quick-footed type chap,
I envied him his craft and his freedom, his knife, his scarf and his cap.
Quietly she sat in the waters, abandoned by a man in his prime,
His legs were entering 'The Anchor'; it was soon on closing time.

He'd be knocking one back in a moment, full of some tales to tell,
He had not bothered to wash or to shave, and people will forgive him as well!
He'll smell not of landlubber's lotion, not what of man thinks girls desire,
But of Stockholm Tar, linseed oil from a spar, and what a man at sea does acquire.

We that sit and wait for our fortunes, to compound in to some form of debt,
Who do we know but the sailor, who worries only how his course is set?
His assets he carries on his shoulder, his future relies upon his grip,
Why who pays more than the sailor, if his concentration should slip?

Down below twixt the oak and pine, would be an Admiralty chart,
With parallel rule and dividers, her last Port-a call to depart.
The smell of a snuffed out oil lamp, hanging on Pine panelled walls,
An eight-day wind-up chronometer, all-essential navigational tools.

Give me the life of the sailor, to feel again what it's like to be free,
Not tied to the land like some Shepherd, with but sheep for company.
Give me a quartering sea, away from the boredom of shore,
Give me my bunch of old shipmates, and I'll never again ask for more!

DRH May 2001

A man's best friend

Through the years of travelling to St Lucia I had seen Gemma deteriorate from a sprightly Alsatian Pup to a sad reminder of what she now was, a dear old thing that slept more than she barked at those passing by. "Well, I'm off to bed" I'd say and her ears would prick up and slowly she rise on tired old legs happy to rest again on my porch behind the safety of the small fence and her younger more "Lets play again?" hounds. How many times I've seen the sadness as yet again my brother has to bury a faithful old friend and it is the very reason I do not have a dog.

Gem

It could be days, it may be weeks, one can never tell.
It was the same with Chubby, and we still remember Belle.
The same will happen to young Holly, and again tears must we stem.
When comes the time to say goodbye, to our dear old Gem!

She is past the days of sit and beg, past orders and commands.
She's done her duty far beyond, anymore demands.
There she lays ears pricked, but there's tiredness in the sigh,
It's hard for her to raise herself, and we cannot tell her why.

How many times has she laid, guarding my porch at night?
I can sleep there peacefully, while she gets some peace and quiet.
Still she may scare off the intruder, by the bark and snarling lip,
But may have trouble catching him, due to her problemed hip!

I've seen you chase the stick old thing, patrol your piece of ground,
I've watched before a younger girl, started pushing you around.
Why it's the same for man or for beast, respect is never given,
For you it's the power in the teeth, for man, the fist driven.

I have a feeling dear old girl, when I come back again,
I may look at where you now lay, and just remember when.
I see the days a-coming, I see the old age in her eye,
So now old girl I am off again, but will this time say goodbye!

DRH July 1999

An old school

'When all has been taken from us - and the new world replaces the old,
When memories are not worth having - and we all do as we are told.
When our opinions are not worth the bother and our betters decide our fate,
When decisions that need to be slept on - you'll find you're one day too late'

DRH

Jonathan my youngest son went to this school, as did his older brother Matthew. They were among the last to leave this fine old building before the Church sold it in the early 90's. The Church was more interested about the proceeds of the sale than what would become of it. Very much like Christianity itself. It would have made a fine Village Hall rather than the new one built outside the Hamlet one half a mile to far to walk on a wet and windy night for the elderly to attend meetings and partake in Village life.

The old school is now apartments - as is the old Methodist Chapel whose once wonderful acoustics made by its high-pitched roof would also have made a fine Hall. I was part of the audience that listened to a play performed there one night, wonderful sound! Now both house the stranger and the ever-growing population in this area.

Conscience (The old school St Newlyna)

In the centre of the Village, made of stone, brick and slate,
The old school stands there proudly, though neglected of late.
Soon to close its doors, let no more children through,
Reasons in abundance, for the wisest thing to do.

There are no inside toilets, no room for them to play,
Parking is a problem too, at the start and end of day.
The building gets too cold, they froze when the north winds blew,
Too cold and antiquated, we could do with something new!

So the sod was cut and footings laid, on the new site they had found,
To move lock - stock and barrel, and the children's happy sound.
But they can't remove the memories, sealed there for ever more,
The sounds of voices of the past, locked up behind the door.

Who will know protect her, when the vandals come to play?
Who stands there to reprimand, now the masters gone away?
Will her windows now be broken, will her doors be kicked in?
Will the hooligans run unchecked, where once was discipline?

Will graffiti be the answer, for some poor troubled soul?
When the Devil points the finger, where the rebel failed his goal.
Are we to stop and shake our heads, in total disbelief?
To suffer shame at what is done, as anger stirs with grief!

I just hope that those remember, when deciding on her fate,
That they were children long ago, at such a school-yard gate.
Where mothers gave you crying, returned happy to their fold,
With stories they remember well, to them now being told.

So be it on the conscience, of those who have the say,
That we alone wont suffer, what they decide today,
That the question needs an answer, not just concerning all,
But the sympathy of a thousand souls, staying after school!

DRH September 1993

Earning or Learning?

Alone the old man works now, to labour and to lay.
He can't afford a youngster, they cost too much today.
Why he'd been on the same wages, for nigh on ten long years,
With all the time 'Redundancy', ringing in his ears!
He couldn't blame a likely lad, not wishing to learn a trade,
Not when a young executive, drives something Italian made!
He looked down at his broken hands, holding a mug of tea,
And wondered where the years had gone, and men for company!

He thought about old Billy boy, how he could lay a brick,
Who shared with him what he was taught, just like any trick!
Between the hods of muck and bricks, you'd learn to 'iron in'
Brush it down, or bag it up, Fletton work within.
He then might pass you the trowel, come the end of the day,
Stand and watch some fun and games, as you did learn to lay!
Yes he thought back to those years, when he did all the getting,
How one day he might be Billy, and another would do the sweating!

Alone the old man sits now, with his silence and his pride,
No one to show his tricks to, no youngster by his side.
Not a soul to say, "He's a clever old sod!" by what he knows,
Never to earn a little respect, for what he shows.
They're out of school far too late, also far too old,
Too big to clip 'em round the ear, and far too clever to be told!
Good boys lost to become young men, caring little for how things are made,
Caring less too about getting a job, while laying in bed getting paid!

'Nice little number'

Oh for a job in an office, away from the everyday dust
Oh for a job that doesn't require, common sense as a must!
Too long he'd been self-employed, no work and you don't earn a thing,
How nice it would be with an armchair and desk, give the secretary a ring.
"Take down a letter Miss Jones!!" I would ask, in a very thoughtful way.
And it wouldn't matter how long it would take, for I'd be on yearly pay
"Dear Sir, the weather outside it is awful; it is up to its springtime tricks,
Therefore I believe we should bear a thought, for the men outside laying bricks!

I've been watching the weather from my window, heavy showers coming in from the west
Its not that sort that says lets abort, but that which causes unrest!
No sooner when they've made the decision, and shout to the hod-carrier 'M-u-c-k,'
Dark clouds appear on the horizon, and words ring out rhymed with Luck!
I see spot boards spewing their contents, all down the 'facework' walls,
And I think I just heard someone shouting, words that could be mistaken for 'Halls!'
So I think it only appropriate, when I watch such scenes as these,
We should leave our sedentary position and be thankful upon our knees!"

'Well?'

Well? - The old man thinks to himself, looking at the sky and the task,
Pouring a warm cup of tea, the last of the dregs from the flask.
Now what was he told as a youngster? words that surely implied,
'Get a trade son, you'll always have work', in one way they hadn't lied,
The problem has been things have changed; they always do through the ages.
But what hasn't changed with those times, is the size of working mans wages.
Tradesmen like us aint protected, Na, not like the professional lot,
They're not paid by the square yard if it is raining, or if it is not!
We can't have a little sideline, like those do who practice the law,
Who develop on land without laying a hand, on a shovel, hammer or saw!
Taking my costs in to consideration, compared to those that make a living in a chair,
I should be paid, by what they would have made, if himself he had to be there!

DRH August 1998.

The garden of England

My sister and her husband live in this county, described once as the garden of England. Though in some places it is far too crowded, one can travel down lanes and meet the prettiest of towns and villages. Far too expensive for the likes of me I might add, yet by being so, it deters the riff-raff of our society. Sitting on the North Downs looking south on a summers day, a soft breeze drifting up the slope and on its air comes the sound of a Cuckoo. Beautiful Kent!

Kent

Have you been to Yalding, where the Beult meets the Medway, then winds its way through Kent to the open sea?
I sat beside that river once, and watched a Fisher be, my sister, her husband, and me!

Where children swam in some lagoon, on that Sunday afternoon, while parents slept in the midday sun,
Two quid to park hence was the price, cheap and maybe not as nice, as some seaside sunny one,
But give kids water and let 'em be, salt or fresh who cared, did we? My sister her husband or me!

Oast sheds lay silent now, the Romany lives in homes, a sign not of how Kent used to be,
No words were said; we just looked instead, my sister, her husband, and me!

Picking fruit or picking veg or picking hops for beer, came the families on working holidays every single year,
Twas not Ramsgate, Margate, Deal, no sand between your toes, more up and down a ladder in between the rows.
How could they miss what they did not have, who would the happier be, my sister her husband or me?

Have you been through Eynsford, and seen the children play, not that far from Biggin Hill out past Shoreham way,
I watched them in the river; it was Minnows soon for tea, my sister, her husband and me!

From Maidstone town to Allington, whose lock stems the waters flow, moored to the riverbank I did see,
Barges that once saw cargo bound, now are homes a family found, whose costs are a but a mere mooring fee,
I though of that time gone by, from such shores I did untie, a period the sailor I would be,
Said my sister and her husband to me!

How many a sight of Kent we saw, from village green to Medway shore, for all that holds in store to see!
Let me look again I say, upon that beauty one more day, with my sister her husband, we three!

DRH August 2002

The Family Photo

Four laughing happy faces sit smiling at the joke,
It tells little of the truth that such a pose can cloak.
It is a picture of an impression, that one wishes to create,
To be displayed for all to see, such joys to circulate.

All across the country, are families in a mood,
Asked by mother "Please!", to show a joyful attitude.
Children bribed with promises, that they all well know,
Will be paid by poor old Dad, who himself was forced to go.

In every home, in every house, in all manner of types of frames,
Sit smiling groups of people, no one knows their names.
Some lay best forgotten, the memory can't be erased,
The family photo where, the father has been replaced!

The yearly event and its cost, is for grandma's joy,
Of mothers happy daughter, husband, girl and boy.
'Tis nothing but a picture, of another price we pay,
A portrait of family, where the women get their way!

DRH August 1999.

Ye Old Kitchen

Upon a kitchen table, stained with blood and wine,
Sat the chopped up Onion, some Grapes still on the vine.
Parsley, carrots, turnip, rabbit quartered for the stew,
Water boiling on the fire, fresh bread in the oven too!

The back door would be open, to give the cook some air,
A chicken standing on the step, having twice been shooed out there.
Old Bob he lay there thinking, his nose across his paw,
One eye on Tom the Kitchen cat, heading for the door.

The morning sun would shine upon, a stand of runner beans,
A garden full of vegetables, from root crop to cabbage greens.
The music was the sound of bees, upon the climbing rose,
The smell it was of country air, the sound of Rooks and Crows!

Upon a floor of two inch slate, slightly worn by endless feet,
Fell a lump of good red beef, still good enough to eat.
A draining board, a Butler sink, water drawn from the well,
A single high back rocking chair, when aching limbs do tell.

On one wall there hung a portrait, of a name long been forgotten,
In a once fine oval frame, slightly wood wormed now and rotten.
Chinese patterned willow plates, of many shapes and size,
Tin plates and Delft-ware, on shelves did meet your eyes.

Iron Skillets hung from hooks, dinner plates upon the rack,
A Burnisher to polish knifes, an open flour sack.
A chopping block held half a cabbage, the other frenched upon the table,
Flour and water dumplings, a small churn of milk with a Ladle.

A single cupboard with zinc pierced panels, for the keeping of specialties,
It is her home, for her eyes alone, no stranger ever sees!
A steaming iron kettle sat, next to a precious Urn of Tea,
A cosied teapot in a tray, expecting company?

The roof was thatch, the rooms were small, warmed by wood and fire,
The walls were Cob, two feet thick, built on stone to dry 'er.
That was then, tis not now, and who's the happier be,
When kids come 'ome from learning, and waiting was some tea!

DRH March 2001

The Modern Kitchen

The house was sold and modernized, the kitchen wall removed,
The range went out an 'Aga' installed, the heating system improved.
Expensive Marble counter top, man-made Marble sinks,
A waste disposal for the woman, who acts before she thinks.

A washing machine all computerized, a front-loading flop,
An appliance of science once started, that must run its course to stop!
Extractor fans, openers for cans, everything at the touch of a switch,
With the guarantee it is far more expensive, to fix then it is to ditch.

Cupboards with doors of Maple, Beech, Pine or Oak,
Beautifully finished units now, for ordinary everyday folk!
A dishwasher is plumbed in, by its cost the buyer proclaims,
It was worth every penny spent, yet it can't remove the stains!

A fridge gives drinking water, as well as cubes of ice,
It stands to one side six feet high, and fits in rather nice.
Every modern piece of equipment, every new costly appliance,
Stands waiting for the woman, trained in domestic science!

Spices, seasonings, Mustard and things, to tenderize the meat,
Stand on shelves ten rows deep, only good with something to eat!
In another door and repeated for sure, are things that can't go rotten,
Purchased to replace, and cheaper by the case, of what you have, but forgotten!

The fridge is full of surprises, one that makes you wonder what is it for,
It is just another cupboard now, a cupboard with shelves in the door!
Somewhere in this nest of things, is what a very hungry man seeks,
But you must wait for day someone invents, tomato soup that speaks!

While the wife eats her lunch at 'Arbys', and 'MacDonald's' entertains the man.
Quietly sits there on display, something expensive spic and span,
That when the children come home from school, dropped off by the bus,
Hungry as ever they search in vain, and the working mother wonders why they fuss!

DRH March 2001

My Wife

Laying here beside me is a face I know so well,
Eyes closed as the day's a-creeping.
She's not awake just yet, as far as I can tell,
So I'll think about her while she is a-sleeping.

I'd like to know the odds, the day that I met her,
Both of us just passing through.
She signed on there as cook, and as time passed she got bet-ter,
Much to the delight of the crew!

It takes a special kind-a person, as any seaman knows,
To toil at a stove in any weather,
In just a rolling sea, or heeled over when she blows,
A cook has to have a gut of leather.

While I watched the compass, the course and the sails,
The crew having been fed below,
I'd see her come on deck, and sit upon the rails,
With a look on her face that we all know.

How many men, get a chance these days,
To see how a lady copes with complications.
To observe how she works, without any pay,
And how she handles the situations?

This girl, this woman, would stick to her task,
Stay to the end by her guns.
When surely another, you wouldn't bother to ask,
For plenty under fire, runs!

For better or worse, in sickness or in health,
Never is asked of a friend,
Far better is the friend, when lost is your wealth,
Yet would stick by you till the end.

Laying here beside me is faithful, strong and true,
Not a bad thought in her sweet head,
With eyes closed, sweet dreams follow the likes of you,
Of how many do you know this can be said?

If all men could have, and hold such as I,
That in to such never a finer woman grows,
There would be no need for cheating, nor tell a lie,
As every broken-hearted person knows.

Laying there beside me, is not the girl that I once knew,
Nor am I the man she first did see,
Once I was a skipper, she was one of the crew,
We lived not on land, but on the sea.

Life upon the land, can have its ups and downs,
Like the swells upon the mighty sea,
It is the wave of despair, that consumes he that drowns,
Yet he can weather all, with the likes of thee.

Now at an age, when your hopes are satisfied,
At an age, when your desires ease,
On this lady's shoulder I've lent, and I have relied,
Never does she wish but to please.

Sometimes as I lay a-dreaming, of the places I have been,
My thoughts again leaving on the tide,
I long to visit all places, once more that I have seen,
But I can't now, without her by my side.

She is now my anchor, that holds me from a-drifting,
My compass to guide me on my way,
No longer do my eyes, from her go a-shifting,
True then it was, and true it is today.

When man sets his course, across the sea of life,
The wind does take him where she blows,
The treasures that you seek, may come in the shape of a wife,
But only if the eye of the beholder knows!

DRH June 1999

Olympics 2000

It is Sydney Australia this time, the land of the Kangaroo.
Of Koala bears, a rock named Ayres, and an Abo with his Didgeridoo!
It is also the land of heartbreaks, great joy and countless tears,
For it is again the Olympics, after four more trying years.

It is Sydney Australia, but as far as I can say,
It could be again Atlanta, Atlanta in the U.S of A.
The reds whites and blues, the waving of the stars and stripes,
Moms and Dads all rooting for, the worst in sporting types!

Swimmers in their new slick suits, girls built in manly shape,
Leaping, jumping gymnasts, imitations of an ape,
Higher, further, faster, feats not achieved before,
Secret taking, winner making, a drug performance war!

Every picture tells a story, but the story is the same,
If you cannot win it fairly, cheat to win the game,
For to the winner goes the glory, a medal plated gold,
While to the loser little, but being left out in the cold.

DRH September 2000

The local

This old wooden building stood on the end of our lane. On occasions when we had bottles to return, which was pretty rare, or a penny to spend, which was even rarer, we'd run to this old Pub for an Arrowroot biscuit or a packet of crisps. From the side door, one heard the hub-bub of men talking and glasses clinking. Old Mr Carver stood on the steps above you, a man of few words, and delivered you a look that said 'Which one of you lot has been up my plum tree? There were no cars parked out side, just the odd bike leaning up against the Pub. Memories!!!

The Plough' c 1950's

Down the bottom of Hickstars Lane, stood the wooden 'Plough',
Long before the brewery built, what stands there now!
It was a shop, when shops were shut, for a youngster and for those,
Not old enough or brave enough, to go where 'Men Only' goes.
Yours was the side door, where the law said you must stand,
Outside wiv ya penny, swapped for a biscuit in your 'and.

"Yes?" said the man of few words, standing eight feet high,
"Crisps please!" looking up the steps, came your small reply!
For some it was their reward, for bottles in a sack,
Empty quarts of Mann's Brown ale, deposits taken back.
Why sometimes you might stand a-waiting, for 'Old Carver' to serve a queue,
Ladies (whose men-folk stood inside), were exchanging a bottle or two.

You were raised near 'ops & Oats', the crop for making the beer,
The smell of it came out the door, and men full of it you'd hear!
In the public bar they was, your dad most likely among 'em,
Not a woman in the place, to distract the old and young-un!
Their room was the saloon bar, with their man on the tow,
Paying more for the luxury too, in shirt and tie ya-know!

Long before the T.V set, kept the men at home,
Long before the old foot went down, about going out alone.
Men met every Friday night, for some varied conversation,
Work and politics, real concerns, about the state of the nation.
Men from all walks of life, that fought in the last long war,
Talking there together, never mind the clothes they wore!

Talk was what men wanted, a chat over a pint a beer,
Talk about the old times, with a piano tinkling in their ear!
Not was there beside 'em, a wife that might disagree,
Having her two penny worth, making a fool of he!
She'd be back at the house, tending the kids and the fire,
Waiting for her man to come home, full a beer and desire!!

Most men that sat in the other place, were under the thumb of the wife,
She would have the half of stout, while he had the hell of a life.
We knew where most would like to be, given 'alf the chance,
In the other side with a tattooed sailor, leading 'im a merry dance!
Those were the ways you saw as a child, and the days of a child are long,
Never do you ever see change as a child, until you look, and its gone!

DRH January 1999

Not as it was

How things changed and all in ten years or so. The old wooden building was demolished along with many of its old customers. Food had entered the Pub served by young girls and the landlord was replaced by a man of less words, a manager with money on his mind when not eyeing up the waitresses. The noise of children filled the Pub and wives eating scampi and chips filled you with a longing for the good old days. Outside sat car, not a bike in sight and in would walk a group of girls unafraid, unattached and underage.

The Plough' c 1960's

Down the bottom of Hickstars Lane, stands the brick built 'Plough'
Why if I was the age I used to be, I could be in there now!
I could sit there with me lemonade, with me mom and with me Pop,
Eating scampi with chips and peas, talking grown up shop.
Men don't talk like they used to now, they haven't got a place to stand,
And the landlord, he aint got time to chat, not with all the food on hand!

Men now sit at tables, with the third wife quietly bored,
Kids running all round the place, food not eaten - floored!
How did all this come about, what shoved the past aside?
Who were the King Canutes, who turned the endless tide?
Gone went the times when 'loose' was the lady, that entered alone in a pub,
Gone on the ebb went the sign that said, 'Men Only' in working men's clubs.

Young girls in high heels and makeup, suddenly were out of the cage,
Men would be chomping on beer and the bit, at one lying about her age.
The swearing and the cursing, a man with his pint in a glass,
Partial and impartial debating, about all from all walks of class,
Was gone! as they changed their talk, when girls joined the company of men,
Now suddenly the lads were dressed and 'Single', ready to start life ag'in!

Things change like many old traditions, when trousers get mixed with the skirt,
And how could a man stay true to a wife, when young girls are dying to flirt?
It became a different kind of ritual alright, a lift home for some from the bar,
And how many ended up on the backseat, with the 'boyfriend' now with the car!
Those big enough were old enough, but the law didn't see it that way,
Then suddenly pregnant and looking their age, the man who took advantage must pay!

Many a marriage was broken, and many a girl that was 'spoiled',
Many an unwanted baby was, delivered in to this mad mad world.
You can blame it on the swinging 60's, for something has to shoulder the blame,
They did blame the bad bad parents then, now, and will again!
But 'The winds of change' they talked about, was a breeze before it did blow,
It blew all we knew out the window, making room for the consumer to grow!

This new way without traditions, beliefs or a family to feed,
Made for many what we are today, an angry, cynical breed!
We see behind every gesture there's a motive, behind every motive there's a lie!
Every corner too has an angle now, and behind every promise you ask why?
Behind every desk there sits a crook, and behind every crook there's a con,
The life you grow up in becomes tradition, and such is that you pass on!!

DRH January 1999

What next?

I thought this about sums up what I think of how things have changed in my country. Wives were always at home and their husbands were the bread winners, just. Society has changed all that, both women and men work and still can't make ends meet! The winner is the Government who can tax both now.

Time Gentlemen Please!

In many a Club once came the hub, of men in some deep conversations.
All were selected by the already elected, from wide and varied occupations.
From mountaineers to engineers, or men with a fine lined verse,
To men with tales of great ships under sails, chosen not for the size of their purse!
There were Empire makers, big risk takers, men with an open mind,
Wild place seekers, and great English speakers, men with men of their kind!

In a working mans club where shoulders did rub, of men with their glass of beer,
What was said came straight from his head, that only a worker should hear.
Whether Mill or Mines where the sun never shines, the need to meet was a must,
They longed for the smoke, a mate with a joke, and a pint to wash down the dust.
What went for the Clubs was true of the Pubs, each from his own type of class,
Whether out of decanter, long was the banter, as it was with the man and his glass!

It was a way of life without complaint from the wife, for more was just drunkenness achieved.
For when men talk of things it is ideas he brings, and another sort of baby's conceived.
Now gone are those days when men had their ways, and women had too much to do,
For inventive minds got ideas from his kind, to make a large fortune or two.
Thus came the machine, which then did but mean, a woman had more time on her hands,
Less hours at the sink, she had more time to think, a job that once was her mans!

While dish washers wash and clean clothes slosh, and a dryer is burning your shirt,
She stands in the shower every day for an hour, washing off yesterday's dirt.
With all the inventions that had good intentions, to ease for the woman her load,
Every new idea has allowed now I fear, but another woman driver on the road.
Unable before to run to the store, where once a store never sat,
Now there's a Mall, with everything an' all, and men you can thank for that.

Did we get quality by giving in quantity, to the female species of life?
Where is the misses with her hugs and kisses, your dear old trouble an' strife.
She worked all day without any pay, much longer than a man on her feet.
Now she earns more 'un you, with less hours too, but still can ya' make ends meet?
What's done is done what will be we'll become, and that my friend is called fate!
Now machines do the chores and as for keeping her in doors, gentlemen it is far too late!

DRH December 2000.

Man's last sanctuary

.
For some of my life I lived in Cornwall in the small Parish of St Newlyn East. This little poem concerns a couple of dear neighbours of ours. While in the garden reading the morning paper I heard a heated exchange of words between them, which was rare I might add. Out of the house came my neighbour, followed by his wife's voice. Some thing had upset her and she was intent on giving it to him. Her bawling got louder as he retreated down the pathway, his response was, 'Bugger Bugger Bugger Grrrrrrrrrr' (or words to that effect) as he stalked to his shed!

For a moment there was silence, then from his refuge came the sound of music from his small radio, followed by 'La La La Tra La-La'. He had a lovely voice, a nice deep baritone sound filled his back garden, totally having forgotten the wife so it seemed.

It struck me then, just how men loved their sheds; it was their refuge, theirs to do as they wished without ever hearing a complaint from a wife. My neighbour was then in his 70's, had worked on farms all his life as a labourer, which meant herding cattle, building barns, Hayricks, stonewalling etc and when calling oneself a Labourer was no mean thing. He was a nice man, a lovely neighbour and I sadly missed him the day he died! I went to his funeral held at the Parish church, it was a packed house too. Many that came were members of one of the choirs he had belonged to and they sang a last farewell.
Very touching!

The Shed

The man of the house when things are said,
Heads for the pathway that leads to the shed.
When things become in the house too much,
He shuts the door on his wooden hutch.
The angry women's spiteful swipe,
Is soon forgotten on a well lit pipe.
While she in her palace does despair,
He sits content in his smoke filled air.

A man with a hammer and a pile of wood,
Some nails and a saw would build if he could,
A home he'd be happy in, with a single bed,
But not with a wife who wouldn't live in a shed.
She wants something finer, bricks or stone,
Thick firm walls, to call her own.
Rendered, plastered, painted walls,
To show her friends, when friends make calls.

Behind the thinness of shiplap walls,
On nails where hung his hand held tools,
He thought of her anger that festered there,
So decided to appease her by mending the chair.
It had sat many years as a job he would do,
Left by an uncle or an aunt she once knew.

Out of those doors had come through the years,
Many such a project that had relieved fears,
To show she was married to a man not a mouse,
By what he had made to decorate her house.
But there's only so much a man can do,
And as the years passed, the jobs he got through,
Then he might sit, just hammer on the bench,
Proof of the pudding, he was working to the wench.

Spoke shave and moulding planes,
Timbers with all sorts of grains,
Awls, Punches, Cobblers Last,
That mended shoes of children past.
Glue, Valves and Rubber Patches,
Rotten wood but 'perfect' latches.
Tins with nails, some straight some bent,
Orders for tools never sent.

On those balmy summer days,
When Englishmen and Aussie plays,
When over joy was gentle clapping,
A Compton boundary missed by napping.
The wireless then did tell the story,
Of the fight for Ashes glory.
Arlott - Johnson clearly understood,
In the language of our motherhood.
There was no accent from the Dales,
Nor hints to say "That man's from Wales!"

No longer is that old man there,
And when they came they stripped it bare.
When she that never understood,
Gave away his manlihood.
Or sold for pennies priceless tools,
To decorate collectors walls.
That shed, his home, is now gone,
The vegetable patch too is lawn.
And when I sit back in my garden chair,
I miss his sounds on the summer air,
For like that English garden shed,
They passed away when its owner was dead!

The great advantage about living in a shed,
Is that you can wear your boots in bed,
Read a book by candlelight,
Not have to wish a soul goodnight.
Walk outside your wooden walls,
To relieve yourself when nature calls.
In fact, it's very much like living on a boat,
Except of course, a shed can't float!

DRH June 1997

When I was bad!

When I was six I must have been bad, for I lost the first love that I knew,
A home on a farm of old English charm, where apple tree orchards grew.
I awoke to the sound of the rooster, I smelt the freshly cut hay,
The song of the Lark in a summer sky, a meadow for my head to lay.
I sat in a manger; I played by the pond, of Minnows and Stickleback fish,
And there I could say, I would be today, if a Genie granted me one wish!

When I was seven I must have been bad, for I lost me a very good eye!
I suffered long for so many years, and looked for the reason as to why?
I think it made me sympathetic, to the so-called clumsy fool,
For anything on my blind side, I knocked down or over as a rule.
I was also called names and was stared at, so I shied from strange company,
So those with complexes, a disability that perplexes, got my deep sympathy.

When I was twelve I must have been bad, for I lost the use of my hand,
The piano lesson would have to stop, and the dreams that my mother had planned.
It made appreciate the good one, and happy I was on my feet,
For though I only had one hand and one eye, the world I could still run to meet!
It made me think before calling, someone a left-handed fool,
For I had to become, with one hand being numb, ambidextrous with many a tool.

When I don't know I must have been bad, for I lost the sense of my smell,
That wonderful smell of a new day, when the joys of your youth you retell.
It brought me the fragrance of the river, of a freedom un-cluttered by needs,
The smell of now not tomorrow, upon which the adventurous feeds.
You were drunk on the thoughts of the moment, and you drank from the well all alone,
You walked with a spring in your step, down a pathway you chose on your own.

When I got older I must have been good, a great change came over my life,
Someone surely felt sorry for me, so gave me a wonderful wife.
She puts up with me and my handicaps, she tolerates what I have to tell,
And only I know how bad it would be, if ever I should lose her as well.

DRH September 2000

Charlie Force

I met this man Charlie Force on several occasions. He drove an old Van in a state of disrepair, wore clothes in a state of disrepair, his hair, wild, and looked scared stiff of ever meeting a comb. He also wore sandals, no matter what the weather. Yet behind all that stood a character I came to admire. It is said 'Never judge a man by the clothes he wears' how true! I might also add - 'by the state of his hair' in reference to Albert Einstein here. I never met Albert but I did meet a man with as many ideas!! 'Why are all the good ideas my ideas, as some I can recall, but when a good idea turns to a bad idea, it wasn't my idea at all'. Albert's idea on splitting Atoms or Charlie's on developing an underwater digger for wrecks, one must judge who is the most ingenious?

Charlie had come to visit us as we toiled at our task rebuilding an old Yawl. We chatted about all the lost chances of restoring our heritage. "Some bloody fool burnt the 'Ada' you know Charlie?" I said. 'Ada' was an old Schooner that had come to rest in the Gannel close to Newquay. Built in 1876, carrying coal to Truro she went ashore near Cape Cornwall. Eventually ending up here. Owners came and went through the years and she became a total wreck, "and what is worse, another bloody fool destroyed any chance to save her!" — Charlie looked at me through his mop of hair and replied," You're talking to that bloody fool!"

The story behind the reason was, the council (who else) they had given him two options, move it or we will, and at your expense. Nice people councillors, full of wisdom and very helpful. What Charlie had in mind for the 'Ada' he would later use on the 'Lyhner', here was one determined fellow to make amends as he said "For what I'd done!" or had been forced to do. He had wandered across the remains of the 'Lyhner', an old Tamar barge (funnily enough) laying up to her neck in mud in the river of the same name. Purchased for one pound, and far away from interference of local councillors, Charlie went to work raising her from her grave. Tons of mud had to be moved between tides till at last as Charlie said "Up she popped, I couldn't tell whether it was the Oak trees surrounding her sinking, or the boat rising!" quote!

The Lynher

From the trees that she was built from, she did rest beside.
Her hull deep in Lynher mud, her frames awash by tide.
Oak and Elm and caulked up Pine, shaped by her makers eye,
Once sailed down with the ebb, in many a year gone by.

Before the coming of man-made roads, before the Tarmac scar,
Before man abandoned the wind, and took to his motor car,
The Tamar Barge, inside and out, did push against the dock,
Awaiting stone for Fowey, or wood beyond Calstock!

Waiting was a way of life, for a Bargee and his crew,
Waiting for the flood tide, or till a fair wind blew!
But waiting aint a virtue, when you're waiting on a load,
Not when now there comes the choice, to get it by sea or road!

The biggest surprises lay in store for a man set in his ways,
And gone is the life he once knew, is the price he pays,
Devonmen and Cornishmen, from both sides of the river,
Would feel the pinch of progress, no cargos to deliver!

He who has owned boats, be it work or for pleasure,
Would not like to answer it, if asked, could he measure,
If on the one hand, stood his children and his wife!
Weighed against another Lady, and a way of life

The price would be an 'Outside' Barge, built in '96,
By James Goss of Calstock, for Gravel, Quicklime and Sticks!'
But now her holds lay empty, and years that way it stood,
No money earnt to replace, what now was rotting wood!

It was old Sam Daymond, who fought for many years,
Against the tide, against the price, and then against the tears.
He never had to make the choice; the choice was for him made,
And with it he lost his way of life, his lady and his trade!

Where once the 'Lynher' loaded stone, out of Poldrissick Quarry,
She slowly sunk in to the mud, overtaken by the Lorry!
And there she sat some 40 years, nature taking its course,
And nature would have won too, if not for Charlie Force!

Charlie Force did sweat, and Charlie Force did dig,
Raised her hull did Charlie Force, to plank, to caulk and rig!
Now the 'Lynher' is on the Lynher, and all must there agree,
If it wasn't for the likes of Charlie Force, in the Lynher she'd still be!

DRH January 1997

The need to sit

I wrote this due to the fact that in Ohio they are hard to find. Walkers should be walking, not sitting down. Well what about the old – or those who may wish to take in the view.

The Bench

Donated by the Parish council, in memory of the dead,
Sit old comrades in arms, to talk over what has been said.
On sunny summer afternoons, on the best in Burmese teak,
The roll call of old soldiers, gets less now as we speak.

Old Percy that raised rabbits, where once he raised a gun,
To fight for King and country, as his fathers had once done.
Rested there with walking stick, his best friend at his feet,
Is missed by those who knew him, when he gave up his seat.

In some remembered favourite spot, in loving memory,
Overlooking Porth Hellick, the quietness and the sea.
Or the view across The Pool, that loved ones did admire,
A sunset over Sampson, and down The Sound to Bryher.

From Promenade to Market street, from Park to Village green,
Not by chance was placed the seat, to enjoy the scene.
The bench to chat or rest awhile, the mind or those to greet,
Was put there by someone who said, "Come sit and rest thy feet!"

DRH July 2000

What happened to gentlemen?

The rules of war changed in this violent land where rebels could not only claim the life of a better man - but today, can still be remembered for their cowardly act! Officers were deemed gentlemen; many wore their uniforms with pride having won the right after years of service to their country and many a hard won battle. To die by the hand of a man hiding in the bushes, was never envisioned It lead to the French following the example by placing riflemen in the foretops that shot Nelson - followed by good men dying by a shot to the head ever after. All countries have men trained to take out the king now rather than play by the rules of war. I can't think of a more cowardly way of conducting ones self.

The Sniper

His Lordship lay shot and was dying, no longer were the rules of war applied,
A country bled its tears then in sorrow, the day a rebel shot a hero that died.
Without rules to govern men's behaviour, without discipline to hold back the dogs of war,
A man on the foretop with his musket, shot the highest-ranking Admiral that he saw.

In the backwoods of a thickly forested country, a Mr. Murphy had Mr. Frazier in his sights,
This assassination of a Sir and a General, showed to all how the sniper now fights.
He takes his aim at the men of honour; he fires his shot to terrorize the troops,
Then flees from the scene of the crime, where men of violence meet in groups.

With a certain cold-blooded pride, the distance of the shot and the 'kill',
He shot dead a man doing his duty, and spoke of the death as a thrill.
Three hundred yards claimed Mr. Murphy, far enough to make his getaway,
But who would take the word of a coward, who fired on a gentleman that day.

Such dastardly deeds of the rebel, proved a point that America eventually got,
The right to bear arms to defend the country, and to argue your case with one shot.
It can terrorize any person into submission, if that person does not submit to your will,
Of those who will pay the coward, the assassin trained for the purpose to kill.

From a depository building in Dallas, overlooking a Presidents motorcade,
They claimed Mr. Oswald fired a bullet, a greater shot than Murphy ever made.
It killed the leader of a nation, a nation that would mourn the day it had begun,
To fire shots from secret hiding places, like Mr. Murphy the sniper with his gun.

It brings nothing but shame to that country; it lingers on the memory still.
How long will it take to cleanse that nation, unless that nation has the will?
Call it fate, call it kismet, call it destiny, you can call it what you may,
But a Nation that lives by the gun, will die by the gun one day.

DRH November 2002

Positive or negative

"I like David but he has strong opinions!!!" I have heard said. Is it better not to have an opinion than cause an argument with one? I have learnt. You can waste a good box of matches on some whose wick does not quite reach the oil! By the way, my wife's flame is burning brightly.

Positively Negative

If you know a positive person, or married to one just like me.
Then you'll know what its like to spend a life confronting controversy.
Whatever the conversation, you can bet on it with your life,
That you'll be the negative person, while the positive ones the wife!
When you're asked for an opinion, or maybe give some good advice,
She'll point what good such did for me, and how she now pays the price.

Around the dinner table, when family and friends come to stay,
You're told to mind you're Ps and Qs, watching just what you say.
No politics, no religion, avoiding all topical news,
Though in between each mouthful, someone's asking to hear your views.
Nod and say yes to everything, for no is negative word,
Then everyone's totally happy, you agree with all you've heard!

Now of all Gods four legged creatures, the Lemming's his most positive son!
For they all march up to the edge of the cliff, and jump off one by one!
It's a single minded opinion I tell ya!, Positive, and they all agree,
That those that happen to survive the fall, will drown in the salty sea!

As it takes two clouds to make lightning, a positive and negative side,
It is so for the fiery debater, whose views he just cannot hide.
For it's only those who disagree, when changes need to be done,
Might just get someone to listen, while the Lemmings still think as one!

DRH July 1992

Never again

I wrote this poem, for as Locke once wrote 'No mans knowledge can go beyond his experience', the experience for some must come about in the form of death for a harmless animal, for some it is the death of all things man or beast and for others, just a chance to demonstrate against all and everything.

Life itself is an experience, and in it I have just rolled along without any great ambitions. Nor, like a rolling stone, have I gathered any moss! Other than a few grey hairs and now with them, I have time to reflect on those experiences. My time as a country boy out hunting for, what I thought would be dinner and my mother's horror at a time when it wasn't necessary!

The Last Hare

It was one of those mornings on a winter's day, when all was still, not a sound!
You raised your head, from your pillow and said, "There's snow out there on the ground!"
Why and how you did not know, but there was certainly something out there,
So you jumped out of bed, to confirm what you said, and were met by a sight so rare!

It was strange to see such a fall as this, so heavy, so thick and so fast,
Quiet and still, a white winter-land, you knew for sure wouldn't last.
Not a footprint was seen, across the green, and never to be seen again!
It was the day before cars, left unsightly scars, down what was then our lane.

Up we rose early my brother and I, for today was the day for some fun,
We were past the days, of the snowball craze; it was out on the hunt with a gun!
Down through the valley now so white, everything draped in snow.
Across the brook, with leap to look, where the trail of a bunny did go.

Here and there, and everywhere, were the spoors of a country scene,
The Stoat on the prowl, the wings of an Owl, marked the spot where a mouse had been!
There was the fox, now asleep down in his deep dark Den,
Been round our estate, with his loping gait, looking for an egg-laying Hen!

Onwards tramped my brother and I, gasping mouthfuls of the morning air,
Hammers back, we were on the track, of what we knew was a Hare.
We had started him up from a bush near a slough, heavily covered in snow,
And off he went, without a shot being spent, o'r the rising ground he did go!

Long were his strides in that winter-land, as he left us far behind,
But he left his track, and our pace didn't slack, for a chase was now on our mind.
Up he stood with his big long ears, too far off for the gun!
Hard to be seen, in a meadow of green, but this was a winter one!

Ours was the story of the Tortuous; his was the one about the Hare,
And on we came, for he was the game, in this rather deadly affair!
Two good miles were behind us now, as were in heaps, our clothes,
For things were getting hot, and we hadn't fired a shot, just a look and "There he goes!"

Skirting the Farm house and barking dog, with us still on his track,
From cover to cover, for a chance to recover, but never our pace did slack!
By a good pair ears and a fleetness of foot, is the Hare only defence,
By lying low, it was no good in the snow, leaving a trail of evidence!

Under the gate and leaping the ditch, it was pretty certain for now,
By the shape of his track, he was heading back, to his home down in the slough!
Somewhere out there he was hiding again, ears back coming to rest,
But out of his cover, too late to discover, I stood between him and his nest!

Sometimes at night when I lay thinking, of that long hot winters run!
I knew for sure, it was my sixteen bore, and my finger on trigger of the gun!
That slowed him down as he came my way, over the brow of a hill,
And the blood in the snow, showed us where to go, to finish off the kill!

I shall always remember that winters day and the thrill of the long hard chase,
That one easy shot, of the last Hare I got, and the sadness on my mothers face!
For gone were the days to go hungry, where such was in need for the stew,
And I guess in a way, it was due to that day, the gun and I were through!

Raised as I was in the country, its beauty at the time you're un-aware,
For me it just took, one last dying look, of the blood on my hands of a Hare!
They'll come the day, when the hounds don't bay, and the hunt is a thing of the past,
But for some it will take, for the habit to break, to say to themselves "That's my last!"

DRH January 2001.

The Village

The village shops lie shuttered, for all is locked and barred,
Ruffians roam come sundown, like a prison exercise yard,
What can be broke gets broken, as frustrated louts do flee,
Leaving a youthful statement, for the elderly at daybreak to see.

The village hall management committee, have a very un-enviable task,
All volunteers never chosen, and never do a penny they ask.
Those who sit on the board have dwindled, for some it's a hopeless case,
And who is to blame but a youth with no name, the culprit no one can trace!

The price of a village copper or two, to patrol the scene after dark,
Would nip in the bud the local oaf, while the fire is still but a spark.
But the law is too busy to watch them, their parents too busy to cope,
The future for some will be prison, while left for some will be hope!

A smelly young youth lies in waiting, looking for that open back door,
He slides over the fence in one movement, for he has done this before.
He does his dirty deeds by daylight; he leaves a certain smell round the place,
He helps himself to its contents, without anyone seeing his face.

All of us get painted, painted with the same darn brush,
The stranger in town is met with a look, 'good morning' met with a hush.
Yet those who know who's to blame, will never confront that fact,
That the child they bore to the world, could ever do such an act!

Do unto others as they do unto you, should we brand the face of the thief,
Should we not know the face of those, who cause us so much grief?
For if nothing is done we'll soon become, a nation that had and have not,
Where all that we had ends up in, a Sunday car boot sale lot!

No shaking of heads or wringing of hands, can make a bad boy better,
No hand on the shoulder of the untouchable youth, just a polite reply to your letter.
Yet an eye for an eye, a tooth for a tooth, and cast the bad apple away,
And the peace and quiet we all long for, will not cost the price we now pay!

While Police drive around in patrol cars, on the lookout for an easier touch,
Speed cameras now do the work for them, for Police work is not up to much.
They get bogged down with too much paperwork, that takes up too much time,
It is better to make us all pay – than the criminal to pay for his crime!

DRH June 2004.

The English

When God made the English, such joy did he behold,
He knew he could not better it, so threw away the mould.
Long had he been searching, to find the perfect race.
And well he knew he'd found it, when he looked them in the face.

The island had been covered once, by an angry warlike breed,
Who couldn't get their act together, without some Roman seed.
But the maker of us all then, added just that little too much,
So popped across the channel, to look at what's now the Dutch.

Just a sprinkle of them he thought, too much would make a Boer,
So he wandered north along the coast, to see whom else he saw.
Pleased was he The Potter, when he met the men of Clay,
Working along the riverbank, known as The Elbe today.

There had those people, made pastures among the trees,
So he knew for sure he would need, a handful each of these!
Though happy he was with the working class, not all was to his liking,
Till he travelled north a little more, and came upon the Viking.

Now the Northman, Norman, Sea-King, call him what you like,
A cup full of Dane too, and a nip of the builders of the Dyke,
Got thrown upon the Potters wheel, with a dollop of the men of clay,
And with what he had already there, he peddled then merrily away.

He felt the firmness in his hands, the fairness in the line,
It could be well unbreakable, totally unique in time.
He tossed in a handful of character, a glaze from the salt of the earth,
To go with hod full of humour, that shows in times of mirth.
Generous with determination, stubbornness and with pride,
He gave them all a heart with a will, with a kind and thoughtful side.

There came a smile upon his face, when the job was over,
Thus he spread them everywhere, from Carlisle down to Dover.
And when other nations saw them, their broken hearts did bleed,
For all would wish to be one, or hate the English breed.
But as it is with jealousy, as it was with Cain and Abel,
All will have it in for you, being at the head of the table.

DRH June 1999